This book belongs to

....

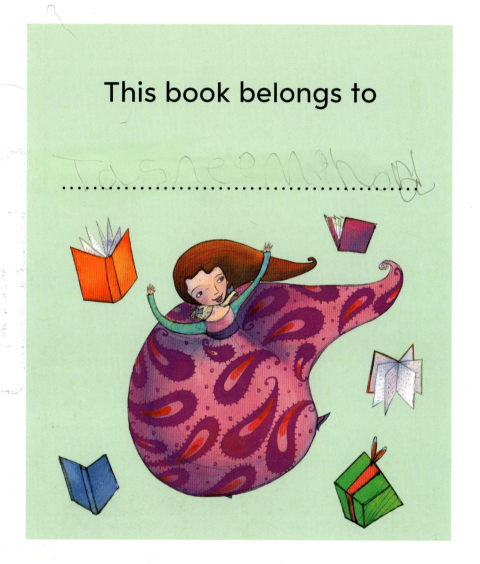

Quarto is the authority on a wide range of topics.

Quarto educates, entertains and enriches the lives of our readers—enthusiasts and lovers of hands-on living.

www.quartoknows.com

First published in 2019 by QED Publishing, an imprint of The Quarto Group. The Old Brewery, 6 Blundell Street, London N7 9BH, United Kingdom. T (0)20 7700 6700 F (0)20 7700 8066 www.QuartoKnows.com

A catalogue record for this book is available from the British Library.

ISBN 978-1-78603-600-1

Based on the original story by Maureen Haselhurst and Barbara Vagnozzi
Author of adapted text: Katie Woolley
Series Editor: Joyce Bentley
Series Designer: Sarah Peden

Manufactured in Dongguan, China TL112018

9 8 7 6 5 4 3 2 1

MIX
Paper from responsible sources
FSC® C104723
FSC
www.fsc.org

Reading
Gems

Story Town

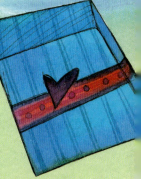

Jazz had lots of books
in her house.

She liked to tell her stories
to the children in town.

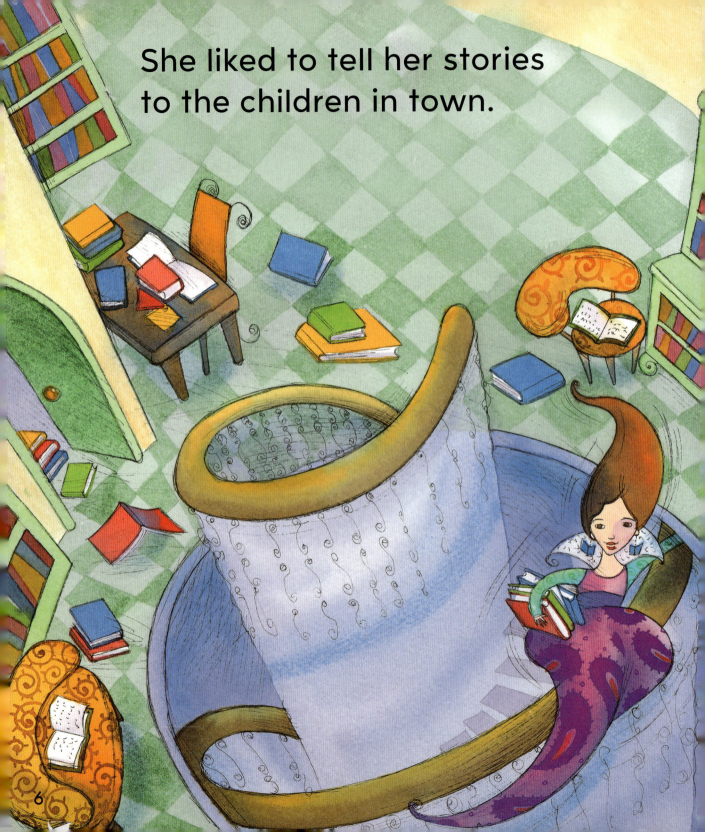

Everyone wanted their own story.

Soon Jazz was too busy.

And she told a story with fireworks.

13

Soon Jazz had an idea.

She got some books
from her house.

15

She got the train to the town.

It had lots of books in it!

She had new books
for everyone.

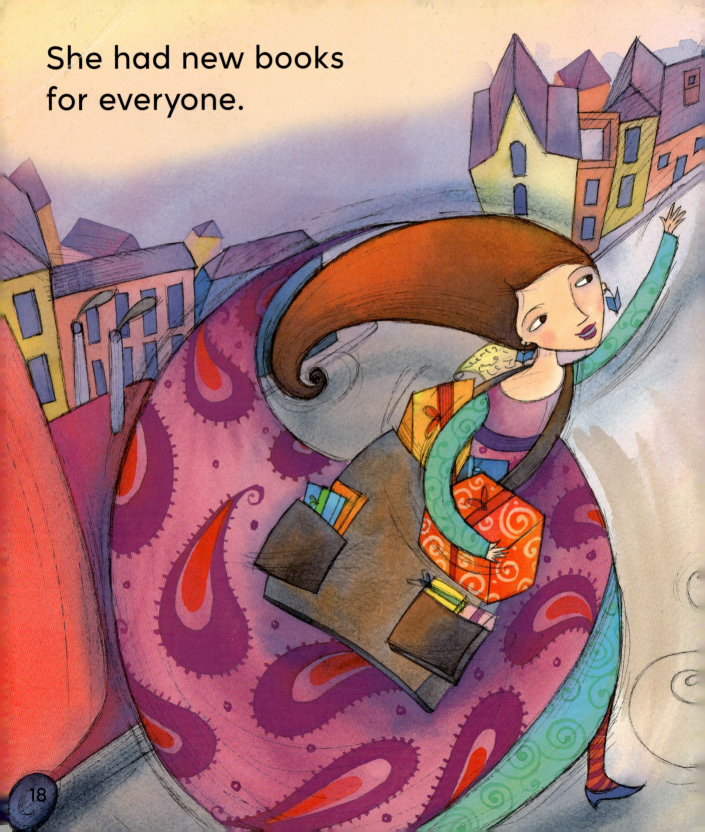

For the children

The children could read
their own stories.

21

And Jazz could tell her
stories to a new town.

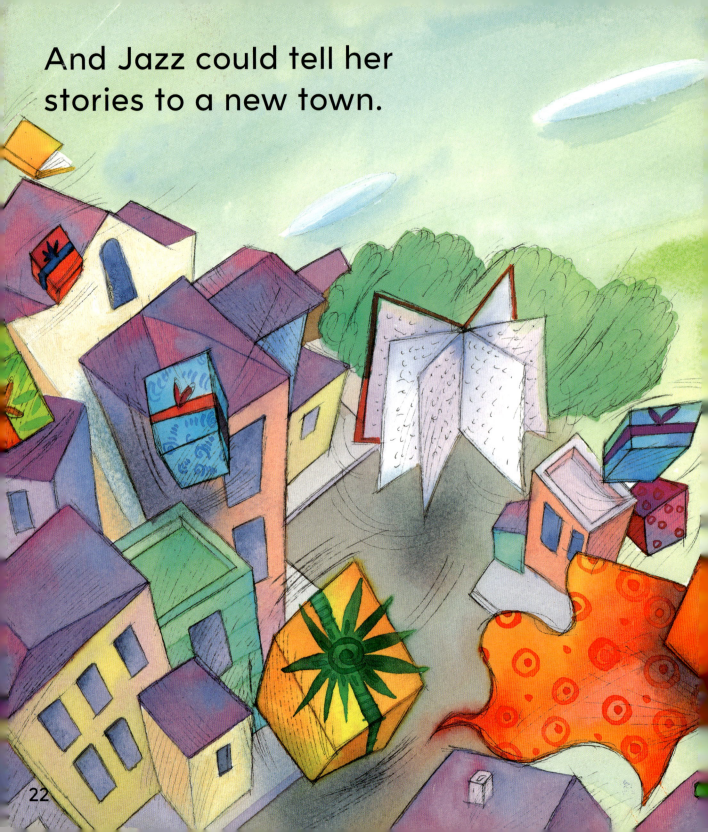

Story Words

balloon

book

children

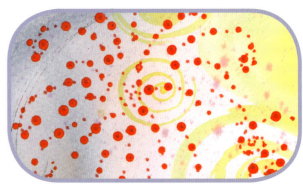

firework

house

Jazz

noisy

read

town

train

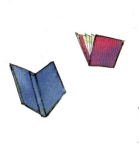

Let's Talk About Story Town

Look at the book cover.

What is happening?

It is a very busy cover. Can you name the different colours and objects you can see?

In the story, Jazz reads to the children.

Can you name the different ways she tells her stories?

How do you think Jazz feels when she is too busy?

How does Jazz get the children to read stories themselves?

What stories do you like to read?

Do you have a favourite book?

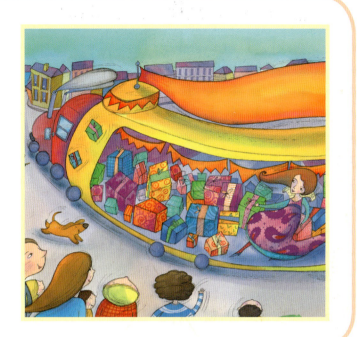

Can you make up a simple story?

Ask a grown up to help you write it down.

Then draw some pictures for your book.

Did you like the story?

What was your favourite bit?

Fun and Games

Find the first letter of each word
hiding in the picture and sound it out.

house   balloon   town   children

Look at the pictures, then complete each word underneath using one of these sounds.

h ai oo ow

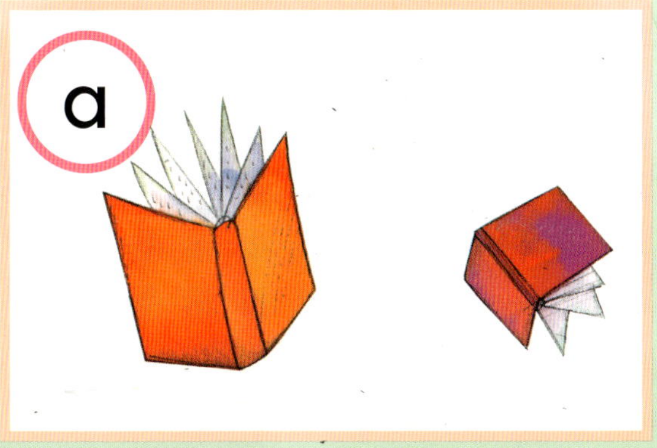

b.......ks

t.....n

tr.....n

....ouse

Answer: a: books; b: town; c: train and d: house.

Your Turn

Now that you have read the story,
have a go at telling it in your own words.
Use the pictures below to help you.

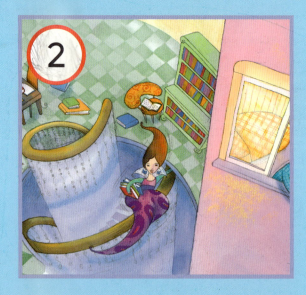

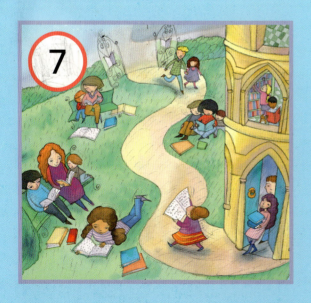

GET TO KNOW READING GEMS

Reading Gems is a series of books that has been written for children who are learning to read. The books have been created in consultation with a literacy specialist.

The books fit into five levels, with each level getting more challenging as a child's confidence and reading ability grows. The simple text and fun illustrations provide gradual, structured practice of reading. Most importantly, these books are good stories that are fun to read!

Phonics is for children who are learning their letters and sounds. Simple, engaging stories provide gentle phonics practice.

Level 1 is for children who are taking their first steps into reading. Story themes and subjects are familiar to young children, and there is lots of repetition to build reading confidence.

Level 2 is for children who have taken their first reading steps and are becoming readers. Story themes are still familiar but sentences are a bit longer, as children begin to tackle more challenging vocabulary.

Level 3 is for children who are developing as readers. Stories and subjects are varied, and more descriptive words are introduced.

Level 4 is for readers who are rapidly growing in reading confidence and independence. There is less repetition on the page, broader themes are explored and plot lines straddle multiple pages.

Story Town is all about a lady who shares her love of stories with the children of Story Town. It explores themes of sharing and problem-solving.

Level 1

Jazz had lots of books in her house.

Short sentences ✓

Simple vocabulary ✓

Lots of repetition ✓

Pictures and words support one another ✓